STEVEN KNIGHT

Steven Knight read English Literature at University College
London before working as a copywriter/producer in advertising.
He then wrote award-winning TV programmes earning BAFTA,
National Indie and Broadcast Awards. As a novelist, Steven's
work includes *The Movie House* (WH Smith Fresh Talent
Award, 1993); *Alphabet City* (1995), which has been published
in twelve countries; and *Out of the Blue* (1997). All three are
published by Penguin. In 2002, his first screenplay, *Dirty
Pretty Things*, directed by Stephen Frears, premiered at the
Venice Film Festival and was selected to open the London
Film Festival, before being released the following year in the
UK and US. The film won four British Independent Film
Awards, the Evening Standard Best Film and Best Actor
Awards, the 2004 Humanitas Award, the Edgar Award for Best
Motion Picture Screenplay, Best British Screenwriter at the
London Critics' Circle Film Awards and an Oscar nomination
for Best Original Screenplay.

Other Titles in this Series

Steven Knight

THE PRESIDENT
OF AN EMPTY ROOM

A Story of Voodoo, Heroin and Tobacco

NICK HERN BOOKS

LONDON

www.nickhernbooks.co.uk

A Nick Hern Book

The President of an Empty Room first published in Great Britain
as a paperback original in 2005 by Nick Hern Books Limited,
14 Larden Road, London W3 7ST

The President of an Empty Room copyright © 2005 Steven Knight

Steven Knight has asserted his right to be identified as
the author of this work

Cover Image: Claudia Daut/Reuters

Typeset by Country Setting, Kingsdown, Kent, CT14 8ES
Printed and bound in Great Britain by Cox and Wyman,
Reading, Berks

A CIP catalogue record for this book is available from
the British Library

ISBN-13   978 1 85459 898 1
ISBN-10   1 85459 898 8

The President of an Empty Room was first performed in the
Cottesloe auditorium of the National Theatre, London, on
28 June 2005 (previews from 17 June), with the following cast:

MIGUEL FERNANDO	Paul Hilton
SIMON	Fraser James
TIMPO	Lucian Msamati
ELENA	Petra Letang
MARIA	Inika Leigh Wright
CRISTINA	Tracey Saunders
SENOR ALLONES	Stephen Moore
SANCHO	Anthony O'Donnell
DONA ALBINA	Noma Dumezweni
DON JOSE	Jim Carter
THE VIOLINIST	Gabriel Fonseca
ALEXANDRA	Georgina Ackerman

Director   Howard Davies
Designer   Bunny Christie
Lighting Designer   Mark Henderson
Choreographer   Scarlett Mackmin
Music   Paddy Cunneen
Sound Designer   Paul Arditti

Author's Note

The typical Cuban cigar factory reflects Cuban society in that it is a mixture of races. There is no stipulation as to the race of any character, but at least half would be black. All characters would be a mixture of racial features, including Hispanic, blond, Oriental, etc. In other words, anyone of any race can play any part, so long as the total cast reflects the make-up of Cuban society.

The business of making cigars is sociable, lively and visually busy. I haven't given exhaustive directions as to who should do what at any particular time, but in general, the rollers sit at their desks rolling, cutting and pressing tobacco with an implement called a chaveta. The sorters and factory hands are more mobile and move from the back to the front of the factory delivering filler leaves. Completed cigars are bound in ribbons by the rollers. Factories are filled with conversation, and so during almost all of the dialogue, there should be at least an impression of noise and conversation coming from the back of the factory.

THE PRESIDENT OF AN EMPTY ROOM

Steven Knight

2

Characters

MIGUEL FERNANDO, *senior cigar roller*

ALEXANDRA, *senior roller/spirit*

SIMON, *junior roller*

SENOR ALLONES, *veteran roller*

DONA ALBINA, *head of company morale*

DON JOSE, *cigar taster*

SANCHO, *junior roller*

TIMPO, *factory hand*

CRISTINA, *tobacco sorter*

ELENA, *tobacco sorter*

MARIA, *tobacco sorter*

VOODOO DOCTOR

VIOLINIST / VOODOO SPIRIT

Non-speaking TOBACCO-SORTERS

Setting

The Partagas Cigar Factory in downtown Havana, Cuba.

ACT ONE

The Partagas Cigar Factory.

It is a July morning. The factory was built in 1845 by people who knew that in order to combat the terrible heat of summer days in Havana, light must be sacrificed. The cigar factory is like a gloomy cathedral. One shaft of daylight illuminates a large painting of Francisco Perez German Partagas, the founder of the brand. Another illuminates a huge portrait of Fidel Castro. From the roof beams there are smoke-stained banners bearing slogans: 'Quality is respect for the people' and 'Nothing should leave your hands that wasn't rolled in your heart'.

At the front of the stage are three desks with chairs. These are for the senior rollers who roll the Lusitania cigars. Behind them and raised up a little is a bench with seats for three people. These are for the rollers of smaller band-gauge (inferior) cigars. There is another terrace of benches behind this one with a dozen seats. These are for the sorters of filler leaves, which are passed forward to the rollers. The cigar factory is laid out almost like a classroom, facing the audience, with the rear benches raised on a slope so that all are visible. Far stage left there is an ancient stove where a coffee percolator sits with some grimy cups. There is also a desk with a very old stereo cassette player and a chaotic pile of cassettes.

The lemony light of summer enters through a door as MIGUEL FERNANDO *arrives early for work.* MIGUEL *is mid-twenties, dressed in jeans and a T-shirt. He is the first worker to arrive and since he is the senior roller, he takes a seat at one of the three front desks. His desk is stage right. He sits down and then immediately remembers something, gets up and goes to the portrait of Castro. He seems embarrassed. Finally, he speaks loudly . . .*

MIGUEL. She said to tell you that she's sorry. She needed to hold some snow in her hand. Real snow. (*A pause.*) Forgive her. Even though I never will.

MIGUEL *turns and takes his seat again. As he does, another young guy* (SIMON) *enters with his jacket over his shoulder. He is whistling. He bows elaborately as he passes the large painting of Francisco Perez German Partagas, then takes his seat on the front row, stage left, leaving one empty desk between himself and* MIGUEL. *He peers at* MIGUEL, *knowing before he arrived that there is some delicate thing to discuss.* MIGUEL *is sweeping up tobacco dust from the channels in his desk and using it to roll a thin cigarette in a paper.* SIMON *feigns indifference* . . .

SIMON. So. Are you OK about it?

MIGUEL. Naturally no.

SIMON. It'll be OK.

MIGUEL. No it won't.

SIMON. Everything is.

MIGUEL. Incorrect.

SIMON. I mean eventually.

MIGUEL. Give me a match . . .

SIMON *throws* MIGUEL *a box of matches and* MIGUEL *lights his thin cigarette.*

SIMON. Smoking filler will kill you.

MIGUEL. Eventually.

A pause.

SIMON. Did you even speak to Alexandra before she went?

MIGUEL. I don't want her name in the air. There's enough dust and shit already.

SIMON. So you made a decision.

MIGUEL. Here is my decision. She is not important. You have your fingers to work with and your tongue to complain about it, you're OK. Another day.

SIMON *decides to try to lighten* MIGUEL*'s mood.* MIGUEL *is hard work at first.*

SIMON. I split with my girlfriend last night too.

MIGUEL (*dubious*). Your girlfriend?

SIMON. OK, she doesn't even know I exist but I was this close to introducing myself.

SIMON *goes to the percolator.* MIGUEL *is shivering a little and seems distracted.*

Then last night I was walking home from Rikki's bar and I saw her being screwed in a courtyard by my own father. Did I tell you she's a prostitute?

MIGUEL (*disinterested*). You didn't have to.

SIMON. You're right. My infatuation with commercial sex has to stop. Either that or I start paying for it. Which of course I can't afford.

MIGUEL *doesn't smile and* SIMON *seems desperate to break through.*

. . . I swear he was screwing her over a fucking henhouse in our own courtyard. Chickens and cockerels round their feet. There were white feathers in her hair . . .

MIGUEL. Simon, the more detail you give, the more I know it's not true.

SIMON *looks a little hurt. He pours two coffees from the percolator. He puts a cup on* MIGUEL*'s desk and studies him close up for the first time.*

SIMON. Are you cold?

MIGUEL. Yes.

SIMON. It's July.

MIGUEL (*bored*). Really? What happened to June?

SIMON. You're shivering . . .

A pause. SIMON *looks at* MIGUEL *accusingly and* MIGUEL *avoids his gaze.*

You smoked heroin last night.

MIGUEL. After Alexandra left I took a little something to help me sleep. A tiny, tiny, tiny amount that Babalero gave me for free.

SIMON *takes this on board with dismay.*

SIMON. So . . . today is 'day one' again.

MIGUEL. I like 'day one'. So much hope.

SIMON. We had an agreement . . .

MIGUEL *gets to his feet, breezily ignoring* SIMON . . .

MIGUEL. You know, last night on the beach I discovered that it is impossible to cry and look tough at the same time. Even if you chew gum.

SIMON. But Miguel . . . you did only buy enough to help you sleep?

MIGUEL. What time is it?

SIMON *checks his watch.*

SIMON. Minus three minutes. Miguel . . . ?

MIGUEL *sets off.*

Where are you going?

MIGUEL. I need a piss . . .

SIMON *dares to take half a step to confront* MIGUEL.

SIMON. You don't need that shit. Why don't you just drink coffee?

MIGUEL *speaks with mock pomposity.*

MIGUEL. Simon, I merely wish to blunt the blade of the day.

SIMON. Let it cut you.

*The confrontation is interrupted by a short, round man (*TIMPO*) who enters with an armful of tobacco leaves. He drops them in three distinct piles on the three desks at the front of the benches. He gestures at the empty seat between* MIGUEL *and* SIMON.

TIMPO. Where is Alexandra?

MIGUEL (*weary*). For Christ's sake . . .

TIMPO. You always talk about Christ. You know what? My grandmother used to tell me, if you say 'Christ' three times in one day, your tongue turns to tin.

MIGUEL (*laughing, incredulous*). Tin? Why tin?

TIMPO *produces a short-blade knife from his belt and begins to cut the string that binds the bales of tobacco.*

TIMPO. I don't know, I never asked.

MIGUEL. How could you not ask?

TIMPO. Because she was my grandmother and she was a genuine witch with four nipples.

SIMON *is relieved that* MIGUEL *has decided to sit down again.*

MIGUEL. Timpo, you are a real peasant.

TIMPO *shrugs.*

TIMPO. So how come my cousin is a doctor?

MIGUEL. I have a theory. Individually peasants are stupid but collectively they are the imagination of the world. Folk songs, voodoo, fairy tales . . . how do you stupid people think up such clever things?

TIMPO *turns on* MIGUEL. SIMON *immediately steps between them.*

SIMON. Timpo, it's OK, he's . . . having a bad day.

TIMPO. You know, Miguel, my cousin works in the hospital pumping sea water out of junkies who got caught by the tide on Santa Clara beach.

MIGUEL. Personally I would leave them for the crabs to eat. Wouldn't that be a sublime death, Simon? Being digested in the moonlight inside a thousand tiny bellies.

TIMPO *cuts his last bale of string and sets off . . .*

TIMPO (*to* SIMON *as he leaves*). He's out of his head again.

MIGUEL (*calling after him*). My gift to this factory is in my fingers. My head is my own business.

TIMPO *leaves. A pause.* MIGUEL *shivers a little.*

SIMON. Why don't you drink your coffee, Miguel?

MIGUEL. I don't want coffee. I want music. Go and see what we are listening to today.

SIMON *gets up and goes to the desk where there is a large stereo cassette player and piles of cassettes. He looks for something on the wall beside the cassette player.*

SIMON. They forgot to put up the rota. I think the boss is away.

MIGUEL. You mean they've dared to leave us on our own?

SIMON. But since music was yesterday, so today must be poetry.

MIGUEL *gets to his feet and annunciates grandly . . .*

MIGUEL. 'Naked you are as blue as a night in Cuba. You have vines and stars in your hair.'

SIMON *giggles.*

I have heard that fucking Pablo Neruda poem so many times it is tattooed inside my head.

SIMON (*laughing*). The factory believes love poems make our fingers more gentle with the tobacco.

MIGUEL. Good rollers don't need to be gentle.

SIMON. We are not all as accomplished as you, Miguel.

A pause.

MIGUEL. Did you ever imagine holding snow in your hand?

SIMON. Is that poetry?

MIGUEL (*softly*). No. It's a question.

SIMON *is wrong-footed.*

SIMON. Why would I?

A pause.

MIGUEL. I don't know.

Two young girls (MARIA and ELENA) enter and hang their coats, chat to each other as they take their places at a long bench behind MIGUEL and SIMON.

SIMON *(to MIGUEL).* Ah! Look! There is Elena! Miguel Fernando, look . . . didn't you ever imagine holding her in your hand?

MIGUEL glances once then looks away.

MIGUEL. No. Not ever.

SIMON. Why not?

MIGUEL. She's too sweet for me.

SIMON. Miguel, you are free now.

MIGUEL. 'Free'?

SIMON. Now that Alexandra has gone. Tonight we will go hunting.

MIGUEL. For what?

SIMON. What do you think?

ELENA comes up to MIGUEL's desk and drops a bunch of filler leaves for him to begin work with. A cigarette dangles from her mouth and we hear a snippet of her conversation, tossed back over her shoulder at her friend.

ELENA. So my boyfriend said, 'I will cut off your leg and beat you to death with it.'

SIMON. You're right. She's far too sweet.

ELENA. You want to fuck him yourself, queer boy? *(To MIGUEL, politely.)* . . . Miguel Fernando, good morning.

MIGUEL sighs as he takes the bunch of filler leaves and begins to examine them.

MIGUEL. Good morning, Elena. How come this stuff is so damp?

ELENA. What, do you sleep in a hole in the ground?

SIMON is passing with some sacks of binder leaves.

SIMON (*softly, to* MIGUEL). There was a storm last night.

ELENA. Thunderbolts all night long. Where were you?

MIGUEL doesn't answer. ELENA senses something is amiss and gestures at the empty desk.

Where is Princess Alexandra?

SIMON glances at MIGUEL then busies himself.

A young girl (CRISTINA) bounds into the factory and twirls her coat over the back of her chair with a flourish. She is almost bursting with the joy of the day. We will discover that CRISTINA lives in a beautiful dream world of her own.

CRISTINA (*brightly*). Good morning, everyone.

Silence. CRISTINA busies herself settling at her desk.

Today is poetry. Am I right?

MIGUEL. Dear God.

CRISTINA. It's a perfect day for Pablo Neruda.

MIGUEL gets to his feet and addresses the factory.

MIGUEL. It's OK, Cristina's not really happy. It's just that she's been watching American TV. Which Disney character are you today, Cristina?

CRISTINA. I was born in the wrong place. You are all pigs.

She glances at MARIA and ELENA and corrects herself.

I am talking only to the men.

An old man enters (SENOR ALLONES), hobbling on a stick. As he talks, he removes his straw hat and blazer and takes his seat behind MIGUEL and SIMON, ready for a day's work on the smaller gauge cigars. He slaps a newspaper down on his desk.

SENOR ALLONES. They are making themselves more unpopular than ever. Like rat catchers.

SIMON. Who are?

MIGUEL studies the smoke rising from his cigarette, elaborately puzzled.

MIGUEL. He usually means the Americans.

SENOR ALLONES. Everyone is happy to see the rat catcher in his village but no one wants to shake his hand.

SIMON. Does he make these things up himself?

SENOR ALLONES. Yes I do.

SIMON. I thought you were deaf.

SENOR ALLONES. I hear insults better than I hear compliments.

MIGUEL. As do we all, my dear Uncle.

SENOR ALLONES. Thank Christ I am not your uncle.

SIMON. Two more and your tongue is tin.

SENOR ALLONES. A tongue made of tin would be useful in this ridiculous country.

MIGUEL. Senor Allones, you have only been here for thirty seconds and already Cuba sits steaming on your napkin like a lump of pork, ready to be chewed up into pieces.

SENOR ALLONES *waves* MIGUEL *away with disgust as he takes his seat. Other* WORKERS *have already begun to file in to the factory, talking, laughing, hanging their coats. A man in his mid-fifties in a wheelchair* (SANCHO) *wheels himself to the second row of rolling benches and is greeted by* SIMON *and grunted at by* SENOR ALLONES. *He looks over at* SIMON *standing by the cassette player.*

SANCHO. Please God it's not poetry today.

SIMON. They haven't left us a rota.

SANCHO. Then I want music.

SENOR ALLONES. No! No more of that Gloria Cubana gypsy shit.

MIGUEL. Senor Allones, you draw an extra pension from the state as a registered disabled veteran of the revolution. 'Deafened by gun fire.' Correct?

SENOR ALLONES (*shifty, probably lying*). Cannon fire.

MIGUEL. Then if you are officially deaf, you have officially no say in what we listen to.

MIGUEL checks his watch and stands up on his bench. He whistles loudly through his fingers to get everyone's attention.

OK, my brothers and sisters in tobacco, another day. And remember . . . 'Quality is' . . . what, Simon?

SIMON (*yawning*). You know I forget.

CRISTINA. He's only pretending to forget.

MIGUEL. 'Quality is respect for the people.'

Everyone begins to set about their tasks, each one of them having his or her own part in the production of the finished cigars. SENOR ALLONES is formulating a response.

SENOR ALLONES. It is true I am deaf but I can still object to certain kinds of music.

MIGUEL. Why?

SENOR ALLONES. Because it makes people dance. And that I can see with my eyes.

SANCHO. You don't complain when Alexandra dances. Where is she?

SIMON pronounces from the cassette deck.

SIMON. OK everyone, music.

ELENA (*from the background*). We want Michael Jackson.

SIMON. And we want coffee.

ELENA. Make your own coffee.

MARIA. If you don't put Michael Jackson on, we'll sing.

TIMPO re-enters with more bundles.

TIMPO. Please don't let them sing.

SIMON. A compromise. Flamenco.

SANCHO. How is that a compromise?

SIMON. Because no one likes it most.

MIGUEL. And if no one is happy then no one is unhappy.

SANCHO. Has anyone told Don Silver that Alexandra isn't here?

SENOR ALLONES *fumbles his roller.*

SENOR ALLONES. Sand and blood and fog.

SIMON. Is he drunk?

SANCHO. Someone should tell the boss that she's not here.

MIGUEL. The boss is away.

SANCHO. Then who is in charge today?

MIGUEL *raises his hand.*

MIGUEL. I will tell him. No one is in charge.

SANCHO. Who is in temporary charge?

SIMON. Why do you care?

SANCHO. If someone was in charge they could decide what we are going to listen to.

SENOR ALLONES. Since Miguel Fernando is the senior roller, he is in charge.

MIGUEL. I am not even in charge of myself, how can I be in charge of a factory?

SANCHO. So do you know for sure she's not coming in today?

MIGUEL. Yes. I know for sure.

SANCHO. How do you know?

MARIA. Because he is the boss.

MIGUEL. OK, OK. Enough . . .

MIGUEL *climbs onto his rolling bench and claps his hands to get the attention of the whole factory.*

Ladies and gentlemen, I hereby declare that this splendid and ancient factory is now a democracy. We are all in charge, OK? My friend Simon is elected Minister for Music and I am elected as President. I can also promise you that before the next election there will be snow in the streets for everyone to enjoy. Thank you, comrades, for your magnificent support.

He sits down again and SIMON *applauds ironically.*
SENOR ALLONES *grumbles half to himself.*

SENOR ALLONES. You are losing your mind, Miguel. (*He
dares to be controversial.*) . . . Over some girl.

An uneasy pause. SANCHO *senses something.*

SANCHO. Everyone knows something I don't. I hate that. What?

SIMON. So Miguel. Did we decide on flamenco?

MIGUEL. No. Not today. Silence today. I am President.

A pause. Then SIMON *spots someone approaching from the
far shadows. He hisses and taps his desk with his chaveta.*

SIMON. Shit. Dona Albina.

An overweight woman in a bright floral dress (DONA
ALBINA) *walks in a stately fashion in front of the rolling
desks. The moment she appears, everyone doubles their
efforts, heads down, silent. We should imagine that perhaps
she is the boss and that everyone is afraid of her. She steps
up to* SIMON's *desk and picks up the bunch of fillers that he
is about to press. She examines them cursorily and registers
neither approval nor disapproval. She then approaches*
MIGUEL *and watches him as he works. She studies him
with professional concern. Finally,* MIGUEL *looks up at her.*

MIGUEL. Good morning, Dona Albina.

A pause.

DONA ALBINA. Good morning, Miguel Fernando.

A pause.

MIGUEL. Are you here for me?

She nods gently.

DONA ALBINA. In my unofficial capacity as head of factory
morale and worker well-being, I have a gift from the
management of the factory to bring you consolation in your
time of sorrow.

MIGUEL *takes this apparent bad news with fortitude. Then
suddenly . . .* DONA ALBINA *bursts into outrageously loud*

*operatic style singing. She begins to emote a passionate folk
song about doomed love called 'Cantata Azul' which lasts
twenty seconds but which is filled with heaving and eye
rolling. The effect should be comical. As she sings everyone
but* MIGUEL *continues to work.* MIGUEL *watches her
performance with a straight face. Finally, her song ends and
she bows for a few moments then smiles sweetly.* MIGUEL
nods gratitude, hiding his amusement.

MIGUEL. Dona Albina, your singing has put my suffering into
a new context.

He turns to the others.

Come on. For Dona Albina. She could eat Michael Jackson.

There is weak applause as DONA ALBINA *exits. After she
has gone . . .*

SANCHO. If Miguel gets a song from Dona Albina, something
bad has happened.

Silence.

(*Speculating.*) To Alexandra . . .

SENOR ALLONES. Let me put him out of his misery.

SIMON. No.

MIGUEL. It's OK.

SENOR ALLONES. It's what I predicted.

SANCHO. Tell me.

SIMON. Alexandra has gone away.

SANCHO. Away where?

SENOR ALLONES. The bottom of the ocean.

SIMON. America.

SANCHO. America?!

SENOR ALLONES. She went from the beach at Santa Clara
last night.

SANCHO. With Ramon?!

SIMON. Shut your fucking mouth!

SENOR ALLONES. Ladies, did you hear that word?

SANCHO wheels himself to MIGUEL, disbelieving.

SANCHO. Miguel, Jesus Christ . . .

MIGUEL. That's 'Christ' twice. You watch your tongue . . .

SANCHO. Last time Ramon tried to reach America he went in a Chevrolet truck. He was on the television news.

MIGUEL. She's not with Ramon. Fucking Ramon?

SANCHO. Who then?

MIGUEL. I don't know.

SENOR ALLONES. Pity.

SANCHO (*to* MIGUEL). But Miguel? You are Romeo and Juliet.

MIGUEL. The Romeo and Julietta factory makes fine cigars but once a cigar is smoked, it is smoked.

SANCHO. She can't have gone. I swear you are lying to me.

MIGUEL. No one is lying. She went last night. They are heading for Key West.

A long pause.

SIMON (*looking at* MIGUEL). In a boat at least.

SENOR ALLONES. Some boat I bet.

MIGUEL (*softly*). A fishing boat. A good one.

SIMON (*angry*). You should have put a hole in it.

MIGUEL. Yes, I could have. But I didn't. She is free.

A pause. Everyone returns to their work. ELENA and MARIA begin to sing in the background, giggling. MARIA calls out . . .

MARIA. If you don't put Michael Jackson on, we will sing a folk song.

*MARIA and ELENA begin to sing a folk song with mock
enthusiasm as MIGUEL rolls his cigar between his hands.
Then he gets to his feet and exits, carrying the cigar. He
exits through a door which opens onto . . .*

The Partagas maturing room, next door to the rolling room.

*The maturing room is a cavernous warehouse next to the
rolling room where tobacco leaves are stored in tercios (square
bales) packed in palm bark.*

*The maturing process is a delicate one and the temperature
and humidity of the room must be kept constant. The progress
of the maturation process is carefully monitored by the most
senior cigar roller (DON JOSE), who is busy checking a bale
of leaves. DON JOSE is late sixties, his skin the colour of
ligero tobacco, lined and tanned, and softly spoken.*

MIGUEL enters the maturing room and quickly closes the door.

*In the presence of DON JOSE, MIGUEL is a different person.
He is deeply respectful, humbled by DON JOSE's knowledge
of tobacco.*

*DON JOSE turns momentarily then returns to his work.
MIGUEL approaches with trepidation and takes a seat,
waiting for DON JOSE to finish his work. Finally, DON JOSE
turns and MIGUEL holds up the cigar he has rolled.*

MIGUEL. Don Jose. I just made this.

   *DON JOSE takes the cigar and examines it. He sniffs it and
   savors the aroma.*

DON JOSE. So?

MIGUEL. I am not sure.

DON JOSE. About what?

MIGUEL. About the quality of the filler leaf.

DON JOSE *knows that* MIGUEL *has a different agenda but studies the cigar.*

DON JOSE. The filler leaf . . .

MIGUEL *(softly, gathering courage)*. Don Jose, I also need to speak to you about Alexandra . . .

Quickly.

DON JOSE. The problem is that the filler leaf has become too acidic. The electricity in the night air got into the tobacco tercios. Many things can go wrong.

A pause.

MIGUEL. Yes. Perhaps.

DON JOSE *gently breaks open the cigar and studies it.*

DON JOSE. The volado leaves are dampened. Also the seco leaves have matured too fully in the fermentation.

DON JOSE *hands the broken cigar back.*

Cigars don't like storms or sudden changes.

MIGUEL *takes the cigar.*

MIGUEL. Thank you, Don Jose.

A pause.

DON JOSE *(softly)*. So you shouldn't blame yourself.

MIGUEL *senses two meanings in* DON JOSE's *words. Finally, he turns and walks away . . .*

And Miguel Fernando . . .

MIGUEL *stops and turns back.* DON JOSE *gestures at a telephone hanging on the wall.*

When my daughter arrives in America she said she would call me. When she calls, I will let you know she's safe.

MIGUEL *hesitates without turning and then he leaves. After a moment,* DONA ALBINA *enters and* DON JOSE *reacts with amused alarm.*

Ah. Dona Albina.

DONA ALBINA. I am touring the factory consoling those who have been affected by Alexandra's departure.

DON JOSE. Please, please . . . nothing extravagant.

DONA ALBINA. I'm afraid I might cry.

DON JOSE. Then sit down. Here . . .

He pulls up a chair and she sits, fanning her face.

DONA ALBINA. Of course I might cry. Why wouldn't I? Even though you and your wife were both atheist, I unofficially made myself Alexandra's godmother the day she was born.

DON JOSE. On political grounds I resent your kindness.

DONA ALBINA. She was such a serious baby. Almost ugly.

DON JOSE. Please dry your tears. The humidity in here is very delicately balanced.

DONA ALBINA (*offended*). Then forgive me for sweating.

DON JOSE. I will forgive you anything.

DON JOSE *busies himself.*

And besides, why would I be sad?

He gestures at the door to the rolling room.

Now she will be free of her 'friends'.

DONA ALBINA. The boys are sweet, Don Jose . . .

DON JOSE. Miguel Fernando understands tobacco better than anyone I have ever known. He could create his own brand some day. Instead he fills his lungs with opium smoke. You know when they grow opium they don't even protect the leaves from the midday sun.

DONA ALBINA. Don Jose, I don't think people smoke it for the flavour.

DON JOSE. And also they say the boat she's on is a good one.

DONA ALBINA. *The Cassandro*. My uncle used to own it.

DON JOSE (*hiding anxiety*). And it's a good boat?

DONA ALBINA. What do I know about boats? I am an opera singer.

DON JOSE *smiles.*

DON JOSE. Alexandra will reach Key West without even her sandals getting wet.

DONA ALBINA. And find work in an office selling cars, maybe. Or wonderful clothes. Those waterproof American clothes that make a noise when you walk. Or perhaps she will become a famous singer too.

DON JOSE. And then some day she will come back.

DONA ALBINA. When Fidelity dies, they will all come back. Like ghosts returning from heaven on All Souls' Day.

DON JOSE. In July you can cross to Key West in a bath tub.

DONA ALBINA. Didn't Ramon once almost make it in a car?

DON JOSE. And this time it's a boat. She will probably ask them to slow down so they can catch fish.

DONA ALBINA *gets to her feet, straightens her clothes.*

DONA ALBINA. So you don't need me to sing?

DON JOSE. No.

DONA ALBINA. I could read a novel. In the dampening shed I read James Bond novels to the girls.

DON JOSE. And how do they like James Bond?

DONA ALBINA. It makes them want to go to a casino.

DON JOSE. It's lucky we live on this island otherwise we would all get what we want.

DON JOSE *turns back to his bales of tobacco.* DONA ALBINA *turns to leave then stops. She decides to raise a delicate topic.*

DONA ALBINA. Don Jose . . . in spite of your atheism, I have lit a candle for her.

DON JOSE. That is very kind of you.

DONA ALBINA. And also . . . I have asked someone to help protect her on her journey.

DON JOSE (*not turning*). Who have you asked?

DONA ALBINA. Someone who will intercede on her behalf.

DON JOSE *stops what he is doing and turns slowly.* DONA ALBINA *is immediately contrite.*

She is very well respected . . . she specialises in the protection of travellers.

DON JOSE (*horrified*). You know better than this, Dona Albina.

DONA ALBINA. Your daughter is in a small boat on a big ocean.

DON JOSE (*angry*). Dona Albina? You have spoken to a voodoo doctor?

DONA ALBINA. I was sure you wouldn't even believe . . .

DON JOSE. Of course I believe!

DONA ALBINA. Then you should be grateful. She is the best in Cuba. The spirits she uses are all pure African. No mulattos.

DON JOSE. There is insanity in every moment of your life, Dona Albina . . .

DONA ALBINA. She is a thousand years old and walks in the evening with a dozen dead children.

DON JOSE. Dona Albina, do you have any idea of the consequences when you meddle with voodoo?

DONA ALBINA (*angrily*). Yes! I do. This woman helped me once when no one else would.

DON JOSE (*chuckling disbelief*). I can't believe that Dona Albina has ever needed help.

DONA ALBINA. I was seventeen.

DON JOSE. And pretty as a flower as I recall. What did she do for that long-lost flower?

DONA ALBINA. She did it gently. She used only her fingers and she whispered into my belly.

DON JOSE *is shocked and stares at* DONA ALBINA.
DONA ALBINA *looks at her shoes.*

DON JOSE (*softly*). Dear God.

DONA ALBINA. And she persuaded the unborn baby to
forgive us both.

*A pause. She gets to her feet. He peers up at her. A sudden
burst of music.*

The rolling room.

*Loud Cuban folk music is playing on the cassette player.
Everyone is working hard but there is visible discontent.*
TIMPO *is delivering filler leaf. Finally,* MIGUEL *checks his
watch, gets to his feet and turns the music off.*

MIGUEL. OK, whose turn is it now?

SANCHO. What are you doing? We agreed ten minutes each!

MIGUEL. Yes we did.

SANCHO. That wasn't ten minutes.

MIGUEL. It was twenty seconds. But with pre-revolutionary
farm worker's folk songs, twenty seconds feels like ten
minutes. So who's next?

MARIA *and* ELENA *raise their hands.*

MARIA. Michael Jackson.

SANCHO. I want to protest.

MIGUEL. Who to, my friend?

MIGUEL *begins to sort through the cassettes.*

SANCHO. We voted for ten minutes each.

MIGUEL. The election was a long time ago. We now all get
twenty seconds.

SIMON *raises his hand.*

SIMON. Twenty seconds each is a good, strong, insane democratic idea. Let's do it.

SENOR ALLONES. This democracy is spoiling everything.

MIGUEL. Senor Allones, how do our political decisions about music make any difference to a deaf man?

SENOR ALLONES gets to his feet and calls out.

SENOR ALLONES. Miguel says this factory should be a democracy. I say it shouldn't be a democracy. So let's vote on it. Raise your hand if you want democracy.

A few hands are raised.

Now raise your hands if you don't want democracy.

Many more hands are raised.

You see? We don't want democracy.

MIGUEL *is speechless for a moment then strides across to* SENOR ALLONES' *desk and slams his hand down on it.*

MIGUEL. But that is democracy, you fucking idiots!

SENOR ALLONES. And we decided we don't want it!

ELENA. Maybe it's the word, Miguel.

CRISTINA. It sounds like 'demon'.

MARIA. There are demons! I can feel them.

MIGUEL *strides in front of the benches.*

MIGUEL. I am the President and I insist that the ancient regime of Partagas has been replaced by democracy and my first referendum is regarding silence. All those in favour of silence stay silent. (*A tiny pause.*) Thank you. Motion carried. I hereby declare that we will listen to . . . silence!

Silence. MIGUEL sits down at his desk. There is an uneasy pause. Everyone works for a few moments. TIMPO stops and looks all around. He speaks in a stage whisper.

TIMPO. Miguel, my friend, this silence is much too loud. Can't you turn it down a little? It's distracting me.

SANCHO. I know what you mean.

MARIA. It's creepy.

MIGUEL. What are you scared of? Your own thoughts?

TIMPO. Silence is the cloak of spirits.

MIGUEL. There speaks the peasant-in-chief.

ELENA. It's true. A thunderstorm wakes them up.

MARIA. I can feel them. There's a ghost in here today.

CRISTINA (*afraid*). My grandmother is now a ghost and I still love her. So I'm not afraid.

ELENA. It's not a ghost, it's the tobacco. I can feel it. (*She giggles.*) It's missing Alexandra. It liked her fingers.

MIGUEL *gets to his feet.*

MIGUEL. OK, comrades, let me show you what it is that you are afraid of. Ready? Here goes . . .

Silence. A long pause. MIGUEL *opens his hands to prove his point.*

There. Silence is nothing. You are afraid of nothing.

MIGUEL *sits down and begins to work again.* SIMON *binds some cigars in ribbon.* MARIA *and* ELENA *begin to quietly sing a silly Cuban nursery rhyme, giggling.*

SENOR ALLONES. Tell them to be quiet.

MIGUEL. Maria and Elena, if you don't stop singing I will have you both sent back to the stripping barn.

SANCHO. At last. Some discipline in here.

TIMPO. In the old days they had violinists. Real people.

MIGUEL. The old days died and are now in heaven.

SIMON (*mischievous*). Well, I would vote for violins.

SANCHO. Me too.

MARIA. When I was seven I played violin for Fidel!

TIMPO. The peasants want violins and they want decisions, Miguel.

All eyes are on MIGUEL. MIGUEL *is unnerved.*

MIGUEL. Musicians are expensive. The tourists give them too much money.

SIMON *shrugs and grins.*

SIMON. If he can find a violinist who will play for ten pesos an hour, will you hire him?

MARIA. How come Miguel Fernando is hiring people?

TIMPO. Because he's the boss.

MIGUEL. If you call me 'boss' again, I will fire you.

SIMON. That makes no sense. Let's make it part of the constitution.

TIMPO. So it's agreed. I look for a violinist.

MIGUEL. You do whatever you want to fucking do, OK?! Jesus Christ!

MIGUEL *crumbles the cigar he was rolling in his hands and tosses it onto the floor.*

You idiots just made me fuck up a Lusitania for the first time in five years.

TIMPO *leaves with a spring in his step.* SENOR ALLONES *is intent on needling* MIGUEL.

SENOR ALLONES. So many decisions, Miguel.

MIGUEL. Go to hell.

SENOR ALLONES. For example. Who will replace Alexandra?

SIMON. You see what kind of people we share our lives with?

SANCHO. The old man has a point. Senor Silver won't want that seat to stay empty.

MIGUEL. And who do you suggest as a replacement, Sancho? Let me guess. You.

SANCHO. Why not?

MIGUEL *smiles to himself.*

MIGUEL. You think you can fill her shoes?

SANCHO (*deadly serious*). I can learn. You can teach me the way you taught her.

SIMON (*wryly*). There will be differences, Sancho.

MIGUEL *reaches under the empty desk and picks up a pair of women's sandals. He tosses them onto* SANCHO's *desk.*

MIGUEL. There.

SANCHO *picks up the sandals and examines them.*

You can see the impressions in the leather where her toes used to be. That's because she was squeezing her toes tight. Because she was concentrating so hard on what she was doing.

SANCHO *drops the sandals on the floor.*

SANCHO. So is that some kind of crack at my expense? You need to have the use of your toes to roll cigars?

SIMON. I don't think that's what he meant.

MIGUEL. How do you know what I meant? If the President wants to be cruel he will be cruel.

SANCHO. I can concentrate as well as anyone else.

SENOR ALLONES. If you move to the front desk it will take you a whole minute longer to get to the lavatory. You might not make it.

SIMON (*turning*). Jesus, what's got into everybody today?

ELENA. The tobacco isn't happy.

MARIA. There's a ghost . . .

SANCHO. Miguel, I'm ambitious.

SIMON. Sancho, may I suggest that you wait at least twenty-four hours before raising this subject again.

A pause. SANCHO *is agitated, suddenly angry.*

SANCHO. I'm ambitious. Ambition makes you itch all over.

SENOR ALLONES. You can buy powder for that. Only in Havana. A little shop that Fidelity runs himself.

SANCHO. I'm owed a chance.

SIMON. Owed by who?

A pause. SANCHO *seethes.*

SANCHO. You fucking kids.

SIMON. Who are you talking about?

SANCHO. Young fucking kids. I wasted two years in Africa fighting for fucking nothing.

MARIA *and* ELENA *yawn theatrically behind his back.*

. . . Then ten years in the hospital. You should give me a chance to catch up.

SENOR ALLONES. Every war creates its own excuses.

SANCHO *calms himself a little.*

SANCHO. Miguel, I know you are upset about Alexandra but when Senor Silver gets back he will advertise for some fucking green kid from the Cuaba factory. Miguel, you could give me a chance . . .

MIGUEL *is exasperated. He stops rolling and turns to* SANCHO. *He turns back again. A long pause.*

MIGUEL. OK. Why not? Come down here and sit at Alexandra's desk.

A pause. SENOR ALLONES *and* SIMON *stop rolling.* SANCHO *hesitates, not sure if this is a joke.*

SANCHO. What happens when Silver returns?

MIGUEL. I told you, I am the President.

A pause.

SANCHO. This is serious, Miguel Fernando. This is my life.

MIGUEL. I'm serious too. This is the republic of whoever-killed-the-King. In the new republic you will become Alexandra and I will eventually become Don Jose and Don

Jose will become Senor Silver and Senor Silver will eventually fall away and die. Like a dead tobacco leaf.

MIGUEL *turns and gestures at the whole factory.*

And Cuba will become America and those little girls at the back will become Madonna and Michael Jackson and the tough boys in the store room will become Hell's Angels with real bikes. Simon, do you like my republic?

SIMON *is unnerved but tries to prove he is keeping up with his friend.*

SIMON. And who will I become, oh great Presidente?

MIGUEL. No one. You will remain no one.

Your hair will fall out and you will lose your appetite for everything and you will sit on the beach. No wife. No children. And your only comfort . . .

MIGUEL *brandishes the half-rolled cigar in his hand.*

SIMON (*pretending it's fun*). Will be a cigar!

MIGUEL. A Partagas Especial Series D number two, rolled by your own hands. That is the only reward in this republic. You smoke what you roll.

MIGUEL *climbs swiftly to* SENOR ALLONES' *bench.*

What do you think, old man?

SENOR ALLONES. I told you already. You are losing your mind over some girl.

MIGUEL. Maybe.

MIGUEL *climbs down and returns to pick up* ALEXANDRA's *sandals. He places them back under her desk.* TIMPO *enters with another bale of leaves. He dumps them on the factory floor. He then grins from ear to ear and bows.*

TIMPO. And also, ladies and gentlemen, I have something else.

He whistles out through the open door. After a moment, a dishevelled man in a crumpled black suit shuffles inside. He is wearing a Charlie Chaplin bowler hat and is carrying a violin. Everyone stops work to stare in disbelief.

I swear to God I found him lying in the alley. Violin in his hand. Like he'd fallen from the sky.

MIGUEL *and* SIMON *get to their feet, amused and shocked as they begin to examine the* VIOLINIST.

MIGUEL. You set this up, Timpo.

TIMPO. I swear on my mother's life.

MIGUEL. Your mother's dead.

TIMPO. I was chasing rats away in the alley and there he was!

MARIA *is bringing filler leaf to* MIGUEL*'s desk. She glances at the* VIOLINIST.

MARIA. I told you there was a ghost around here. He is a voodoo spirit.

SIMON *smells the* VIOLINIST*'s breath.*

SIMON. The only spirit this guy's got is Havana Rum.

MIGUEL (*to the* VIOLINIST). What's your name?

TIMPO. I don't think he talks.

MARIA. Voodoo spirits can only speak to people they love.

SIMON. He's too drunk.

MIGUEL. Can he play?

TIMPO. He's got a violin.

MIGUEL. Simon has got a dick, that doesn't mean he knows what to do with it.

SIMON. Fuck you.

ELENA. Mr President. Maria wants him out of here. He's scaring us.

MIGUEL. He's a musician, for Christ's sake. He's lying drunk in the alley because the tourists give him ten Yankee dollars for two Cuban minutes. Will you play for ten pesos an hour?

The VIOLINIST *nods his head.* MIGUEL *nods with him.*

You are willing to take a pay cut for your poor countrymen.

MIGUEL *slaps him on the back and straightens him up a little.*

Then OK then! What kind of music do you play?

ELENA. Michael Jackson!

MIGUEL. Do you play Michael Jackson?

SANCHO. Forget that shit, let him play some of the old songs. Revolution songs. It'll be like it used to be. Right, old man?

SENOR ALLONES *is peering at the* VIOLINIST.

SENOR ALLONES. I've never seen him before.

MIGUEL. Shit, I forgot to take a vote.

MIGUEL *leaps onto his desk.*

All those who want to hear the revolutionary violinist raise your hands . . .

MIGUEL *doesn't even wait.*

Carried unanimously. OK, let's hear a song about Cuba . . . a tiny ulcer in the belly of America.

MIGUEL *and* SIMON *return to their benches.* TIMPO *takes a seat on a bale of tobacco and lights a pipe. The* VIOLINIST *puts his violin to his shoulder and begins to play a beautiful slow waltz. As he does, the lights fade in the rolling room apart from a single spotlight which illuminates the* VIOLINIST. *Meanwhile, the lights fade up in . . .*

The maturing room.

DON JOSE *is sitting on a hard-backed chair. Only the* VIOLINIST *is visible in his shaft of light in the room next door and his music fills both rooms.* DON JOSE *listens to the music and smiles. He then takes a Partagas cigar from his top pocket. He scratches off the cap of the cigar and lights a Zippo lighter. He is about to light the cigar when a beautiful dark-haired woman in her twenties enters the room unseen. This is* ALEXANDRA. *She casually begins to inspect the leaves. After a moment,* DON JOSE *turns and sees her. He leaps to his feet.*

DON JOSE. Alexandra?!

She doesn't turn. DON JOSE *steps closer then hesitates.*

Is that really you?

Finally, she turns and smiles. DON JOSE *looks at her and realises something. He lays his cigar aside.*

(*Angry.*) You are a spirit.

ALEXANDRA. More than that, Papa.

DON JOSE. You are voodoo and I want nothing to do with you. You should see Dona Albina. She is paying the bill.

ALEXANDRA. Smoke your cigar, Papa.

DON JOSE. I won't have spirits in my factory. You spoil the tobacco.

A pause.

ALEXANDRA. Don't you want to know where I am?

The VIOLINIST *continues to play and the music sweeps.* DON JOSE *resists the temptation to speak to* 'ALEXANDRA' *for a while . . . then he looks at her open smile and can't help himself.*

DON JOSE. Are you safe, Alexandra?

ALEXANDRA. We are still at sea, Papa. No sight of land yet.

DON JOSE. Can I look?

She shrugs. DON JOSE *joins her, puts his arm around her waist and they both peer at one of the walls of the gloomy maturing room. Suddenly the wall falls away and bright sunlight floods the room. They take a single step towards it, their faces bathed in light.*

ALEXANDRA. You see America, Papa?

DON JOSE. Oh Alexandra.

ALEXANDRA. It's just there.

DON JOSE. The Gulf of Mexico was a prison wall for you.

ALEXANDRA. A garden fence. I just wanted to leave our
beautiful garden.

DON JOSE. It is a good boat, isn't it?

ALEXANDRA. Instead of Alexandra, why didn't you call me
'Dolphin'?

DON JOSE. Dolphin?

ALEXANDRA. Then I could swim.

DON JOSE. Because we hoped you would stay.

ALEXANDRA. How is poor Miguel Fernando?

DON JOSE. I hear he has declared himself President of what's
left.

ALEXANDRA. As if that's very little.

DON JOSE. It is very little. For me it's nothing.

ALEXANDRA *turns to him.*

ALEXANDRA. You always said you wanted me to leave some
day.

DON JOSE. You are voodoo. So I must tell you the truth. In
my heart I wanted you to stay. For my own happiness. Even
if it made you unhappy. I am selfish.

ALEXANDRA *turns away from the light.*

ALEXANDRA. The boat is fine. It's going to be OK. We will
reach Key West in six hours.

DON JOSE. The weather is good?

ALEXANDRA. There is a storm but we are ahead of it.

DON JOSE. Good. So you are safe. In the end that's all that
matters.

ALEXANDRA *kisses him on both cheeks and leaves.* DON JOSE *sits down sadly and the slow waltz ends. The* VIOLINIST *suddenly begins to play a fast tango and the lights in the maturing room fade. The lights go up in what was the rolling room but which has now been transformed into the factory courtyard.*

The courtyard of the Partagas factory.

The courtyard has high walls, with tobacco bales stacked in the shade. The FACTORY WORKERS *are all gathered in a semi-circle and the* VIOLINIST *walks to the centre of the crowd, playing at a fiery tempo. Some of the* WORKERS *are dancing, others clapping and cheering.* MIGUEL *is leading the clapping.* SIMON *approaches* MIGUEL *and takes him aside.*

SIMON. Miguel Fernando, are you sure this is a good idea?

MIGUEL. It's our lunch break, we can do what we want.

SIMON. What will Don Silver say?

MIGUEL. Don Silver isn't here.

SIMON. When he returns.

MIGUEL. We will tell him this guy can really play!

MIGUEL *calls out to the* VIOLINIST.

Hey! Play something boring. My friend here wants to dance. Play something fast and he gets scared.

SIMON. I don't dance.

MIGUEL. You don't dance, you don't fuck . . .

SIMON *tries to pull him away a little.*

SIMON. Miguel, come on . . . Alexandra leaves and you fall to pieces . . .

MIGUEL. I like being in pieces. Every piece is happy.

SIMON. There is more heroin in your eyes. You've smoked again today . . .

MIGUEL. Hey Simon, you should remember that I am the boss around here . . .

SIMON. Miguel, I know you are joking but some of the young ones are beginning to believe it. They think you're really in charge.

MIGUEL. I am in charge. Dona Albina! Will you dance with me?

DONA ALBINA *steps out from the crowd and bows elaborately.* SANCHO *looks on, delighted.*

DONA ALBINA. It would be a pleasure. What shall we dance?

MIGUEL. Flamenco!

DONA ALBINA. I don't dance flamenco.

MIGUEL. Neither do I but you just clap your hands and shout out whatever comes into your head.

SANCHO. That's not true. You shout out whatever is in your heart. It's called the cantata.

MIGUEL. So OK, that's even more embarrassing! Good. Come on.

The VIOLINIST *begins to play a slow and rhythmic dirge.* MIGUEL *is mocking the mood, stamping his feet with vastly overblown movements, his face a picture of wounded love.* DONA ALBINA *is equally wounded, but her passion is genuine. The two dancers approach front of stage and hiss to each other in a subdued rendition of the classic cantata style.*

(*Mocking.*) Oh Alexandra, my love. Why did you leave me?

DONA ALBINA. Oh Don Jose, my little bird. Why didn't I tell you the truth all those years ago?

They turn and dance back into the crowd who watch with amusement. They turn again and come to front of stage.

MIGUEL. Alexandra, you left me crying on the beach . . . like a . . . like a . . . Brazilian soap-opera star.

DONA ALBINA. I flicker like a candle when I think of how he might have divorced that bitch and married me.

They turn and MIGUEL *sweeps* DONA ALBINA *into his arms.*

MIGUEL. Perhaps Alexandra is a swallow who will return some day.

They dance some more. MIGUEL *breaks away and addresses* SIMON *directly as the music continues.*

You see. The music makes fun of us whether we dance to it or not.

DONA ALBINA *joins* MIGUEL *and sighs.*

DONA ALBINA. One thing I know to be true, Miguel. You cannot escape from the fat woman in the mirror.

MIGUEL. Except through music and wine.

DONA ALBINA. If I were to be made into a wine, the wine would be called 'She sacrificed herself for Don Jose'. Or something like that.

MIGUEL. If I were to be made into a wine . . .

He thinks. He mocks himself with a grand gesture . . .

'He was too afraid of her beauty.'

DONA ALBINA. I hate beauty because I used to be beautiful.

MIGUEL. Dona Albina, I should have burnt Alexandra's boat last night.

DONA ALBINA. You should have. We have a duty to keep the beautiful people here.

MIGUEL. I would have done it! I had the chance. I was on the beach with her and I had matches and oil.

DONA ALBINA. But no violin.

MIGUEL. So I wished the boat well and walked home. Like a coward.

DONA ALBINA *turns around and spots someone in the crowd . . .*

DONA ALBINA. Ah . . . but look, Miguel Fernando . . . look what the music has done.

From among the young girls, ALEXANDRA *emerges and holds out her hand to* MIGUEL *for him to dance.* MIGUEL *steps back in total amazement. He stops and stares, his wild bad humour dissipated. It seems that only he and* DONA ALBINA *can see* ALEXANDRA. MIGUEL *turns to* DONA ALBINA.

MIGUEL. Do you see her too?

DONA ALBINA. Dance with her. She is real for you.

DONA ALBINA *urges* MIGUEL *to step forward and he takes* ALEXANDRA's *hand. The violin music sweeps into a waltz again and* DONA ALBINA *puts her handkerchief to her eyes and retires.* MIGUEL *and* ALEXANDRA *dance the waltz, and this time* MIGUEL's *emotion is real. As they dance, the rest of the* WORKERS *chat and smoke. The music softens and* MIGUEL *stares into* ALEXANDRA's *eyes.*

MIGUEL. Alexandra, have you come back to me?

ALEXANDRA *and* MIGUEL's *eyes are locked together but she doesn't speak. Then she turns and flees through the door of the maturing room, which is darkness.* MIGUEL *is left alone. He stares at the door for a long time.* DONA ALBINA *comes to his shoulder and whispers.*

DONA ALBINA. It's OK, Miguel Fernando. You can follow her.

MIGUEL. Is she real? . . .

DONA ALBINA. It doesn't matter. There is someone holding the door for you. Go . . .

MIGUEL *hesitantly walks towards the door. The waltz comes to an end and all is silent.* DONA ALBINA *hisses at* MIGUEL *once more.*

Go . . .

MIGUEL *walks through the door into darkness.*

ACT TWO

The maturing room in a pale-blue half-light.

DON JOSE *is asleep in a chair beside a small table and a bale of tobacco. From the half-darkness at the back of the stage* ALEXANDRA *emerges, carrying a long cigar and a Zippo lighter. She comes to* DON JOSE's *side and smells the cigar, savouring it. She gently strokes* DON JOSE's *hair then flicks the Zippo alight and begins to light the cigar without putting it to her lips. Finally, the cigar begins to smoulder and she wafts it under* DON JOSE's *nose like smelling salts. As he begins to stir,* ALEXANDRA *puts the cigar carefully onto the table, flicks the lighter closed, and walks slowly away off stage. As* DON JOSE *opens his eyes,* MIGUEL *suddenly bursts in . . .*

MIGUEL. Alexandra?!

> *A pause.* MIGUEL *looks all around, breathing hard. He sees no one but* DON JOSE. MIGUEL *stops dead in his tracks.* DON JOSE *chuckles as he sits up and carefully examines the lit cigar.*

DON JOSE. Are you looking for someone?

> MIGUEL *hesitates.*

MIGUEL. No, no . . . no one.

> DON JOSE *begins to release large blinds which allow more light into the maturing room as he takes a drag on the cigar and blows blue smoke into the new light.* MIGUEL *is still staring all around.* DON JOSE *examines him.*

DON JOSE. You saw Alexandra?

MIGUEL. No. How could I? She is on a boat in the Gulf of Mexico.

DON JOSE. Even so, you saw her.

> DON JOSE *returns to his chair.*

You think perhaps she was an hallucination caused by the opium you've smoked . . .

MIGUEL *reacts to* DON JOSE*'s knowledge.*

But in fact it is something much stronger than heroin.

MIGUEL. Don Jose, did you see Alexandra?

DON JOSE *tastes the smoke with professional concern.*

DON JOSE. Have you noticed, Miguel, that the filler Don Silver is buying is inferior quality? That they are sending binder leaf from Guantanamo Bay?

MIGUEL. Don Jose, what is happening? I think I am going insane.

DON JOSE *takes a seat and studies the cigar.*

DON JOSE. Dona Albina has engaged the services of a voodoo doctor. Strange things will happen.

MIGUEL *looks spooked.*

MIGUEL. Voodoo is just pins and rum.

DON JOSE. You know as well as I do that voodoo means truth.

MIGUEL. Truth?

DON JOSE. What did you see?

MIGUEL. I saw Alexandra dancing. I danced with her.

DON JOSE. Did she speak to you?

MIGUEL. No.

A pause. DON JOSE *looks up at* MIGUEL.

DON JOSE. I saw something different.

MIGUEL. Tell me.

DON JOSE. Tobacco leaves. A little girl hiding among the tobacco leaves. A birthday party. She wore a dress the colour of green tobacco and so we couldn't find her all afternoon. Just when I began to worry that she was really lost she stood up and waved at me.

DON JOSE *offers the cigar to* MIGUEL.

Voodoo truth is a blend of memory and hope. Like a good Lusitania cigar.

MIGUEL *hesitates.*

MIGUEL. Don Jose . . . you only ever smoke when you are alone.

DON JOSE. Today I am not smoking. I am praying. My grandmother was an Indian.

A pause.

MIGUEL. Mine too.

DON JOSE *urges* MIGUEL *to take the cigar and finally he takes it like a pipe of peace.*

DON JOSE. Perhaps that is why we see the visions so easily.

MIGUEL *draws in some smoke and lets the smoke soothe him.*

MIGUEL. Are we praying for the same thing?

DON JOSE *chuckles.*

DON JOSE. I am simply praying for the thing every parent prays for. That my child left home on board a good boat.

A pause. MIGUEL *hands the cigar back.* DON JOSE *lays the cigar aside and closes his eyes.*

Now I'd like you to leave me to pray on my own.

A pause. MIGUEL *gets to his feet and hesitates.*

MIGUEL. Don Jose, did she ever talk to you about me?

A pause. DON JOSE *doesn't open his eyes.*

DON JOSE. No. Never.

MIGUEL *wants to ask more but turns to leave. As he walks away . . .*

(Eyes closed.) Straighten yourself out, Miguel. Create some beautiful new cigar.

MIGUEL *stops.*

MIGUEL. Why not, Don Jose? I could call it 'Alexandra'.
Then old men all over the world could put her to their lips.

   MIGUEL *exits into . . .*

The rolling room.

MIGUEL *goes to his desk and sits down, staring straight*
ahead. From outside we can hear the sound of violin music
and WORKERS *clapping and dancing in the courtyard.*
MIGUEL *looks around at the empty benches. He shivers a*
little, shoves his hands into his armpits. SIMON *enters.*

SIMON. They are still dancing out there.

   MIGUEL *feigns brightness.*

MIGUEL. Today is the feast day of St Vitus, the patron saint
of dancing. In Catholic countries the workers are allowed to
dance all afternoon.

SIMON. Is that true?

MIGUEL. Of course it's not fucking true but I am the
President, so . . . it is true.

   MIGUEL *rubs his face wearily.* SIMON *peers at him.*
   MIGUEL *slams his hand down on the desk.*

   Simon! Stop looking at me! It's like you are always waiting
   for something!

   SIMON *gets to his feet.*

SIMON. I am. I am waiting for 'day two'.

   SIMON *turns to leave.* MIGUEL *turns.*

MIGUEL. That's right, go. Go and learn to dance or drink or
fuck or something. Don't just look.

   SIMON *leaves.* MIGUEL *is alone. He immediately regrets*
   what he said. After a moment SENOR ALLONES *enters*

with a rolled-up newspaper under his arm. He walks past
MIGUEL*'s bench primly.*

SENOR ALLONES. Since you are in charge, Miguel Fernando,
you should know that the shit-house door is hanging on by
a single screw.

MIGUEL (*watching him pass*). Well, since you mention it,
Senor Allones, my mind is hanging on by a single screw.
Which screw should I deal with first?

SENOR ALLONES. You're the boss.

SENOR ALLONES *continues to walk towards the maturing
room and* MIGUEL *seems puzzled.*

MIGUEL. Senor Allones, where are you going?

SENOR ALLONES *is filled with portent.*

SENOR ALLONES. To talk to Don Jose.

MIGUEL *gets to his feet in amazement.*

MIGUEL. But you don't speak to Don Jose. And he doesn't
speak to you.

SENOR ALLONES *straightens his collar as he prepares to
go through the door.*

SENOR ALLONES. Today is an unusual day.

He passes through the door into . . .

The maturing room.

DON JOSE *is sitting in his chair, asleep.* SENOR ALLONES
enters and hesitates. Finally, he clears his throat. DON JOSE
is awake but pretends to be asleep. Finally . . .

SENOR ALLONES. Don Jose.

DON JOSE *remains 'asleep'.* SENOR ALLONES *hesitates
then takes a seat on a bale of tobacco. He sniffs the air.*

From the smell of the smoke I would say you have been smoking a Partagas Series D. Rolled this morning.

DON JOSE *keeps his eyes closed.*

DON JOSE. No. The aroma you smell in the air is my daughter's perfume. Now if you don't mind, I am asleep.

DON JOSE *appears to sleep. A pause.* SENOR ALLONES *wants conversation.*

SENOR ALLONES. Sleep. If only. I dream of sleep.

DON JOSE *opens his eyes.*

DON JOSE. You have insomnia?

SENOR ALLONES. Whatever it is I have, it is stopping me from sleeping.

DON JOSE *finally sighs, stands and stretches. He turns his back to the audience and apparently urinates onto a bale of tobacco.* SENOR ALLONES *turns, surprised.*

DON JOSE. For the diplomatic consignment. I hate all politicians. And yet they always come back for more.

SENOR ALLONES. You know it's sad . . .

DON JOSE. Of course it's sad.

SENOR ALLONES. But I predicted it.

DON JOSE. You predicted everything. But only after it happened.

DON JOSE *finishes peeing and sits down again.*

SENOR ALLONES. Alexandra inherited her spirit from her mother.

DON JOSE. 'Spirit'?

SENOR ALLONES. Her desire to escape.

DON JOSE. Her mother escaped.

SENOR ALLONES. She contracted cancer because she was in a cage.

DON JOSE. Made by my own fair hands.

SENOR ALLONES. What I mean is . . . Alexandra's spirit should have been tempered by my . . .

DON JOSE. By your what?

SENOR ALLONES. By my . . . lack of spirit.

A pause.

DON JOSE. You mean if Alexandra's mother had married you instead of me.

SENOR ALLONES. Yes. Precisely.

DON JOSE. But if you had been Alexandra's father she wouldn't have been Alexandra.

SENOR ALLONES. You always were in a hurry to introduce philosophy into simple matters.

DON JOSE *produces a bottle of tequila from his pocket, raises it to no one and swigs.*

DON JOSE. To calmness in the Gulf between father and daughter.

SENOR ALLONES. She would have learnt my . . .

DON JOSE. Laziness.

SENOR ALLONES. Exactly. On an island this small, laziness is important.

DON JOSE. Vital.

SENOR ALLONES. Essential.

DON JOSE. You're right. My wife should have married you. You loved her more than I did.

SENOR ALLONES. I want some tequila.

DON JOSE *hands him the bottle and* SENOR ALLONES *swigs.*

DON JOSE. You idiots and your love.

SENOR ALLONES. Without love, what?

DON JOSE. Common sense.

SENOR ALLONES. Do you use common sense when you select tobacco.

A pause.

DON JOSE. That's different.

SENOR ALLONES. You love Alexandra.

A pause. DON JOSE *takes the bottle of tequila back and raises a toast.*

DON JOSE. To her. Only.

He drinks.

Why are you in here anyway?

SENOR ALLONES. This is an unusual day.

DON JOSE. How long is it since we spoke to each other?

SENOR ALLONES. I forget.

DON JOSE. Well, I don't. It is at least eight years.

SENOR ALLONES. Eight-and-a-half.

DON JOSE. Can you remember what we quarrelled about?

SENOR ALLONES (*indignant*). Yes.

DON JOSE. What?

SENOR ALLONES. Tobacco.

DON JOSE. Well, of course tobacco but what in particular?

A pause. Finally . . .

SENOR ALLONES. I forget.

DON JOSE. Then let's both forget. We're too old to be jagged. We have been smoothed by time.

SENOR ALLONES. Two pebbles in a pocket.

DON JOSE. Very good. You know, I remember now that once upon a time I liked you.

SENOR ALLONES. You must have a good memory.

DON JOSE. You could have the decency to say that once upon a time you also liked me.

SENOR ALLONES. It wouldn't be true.

DON JOSE. This is a reconciliation. What's so special about the truth?

SENOR ALLONES. There. Now you have it.

SENOR ALLONES shifts uncomfortably.

DON JOSE. Now I have what?

SENOR ALLONES. The reason I am here. Talking to you. I am here about . . . the truth.

DON JOSE peers at SENOR ALLONES and nods slowly.

DON JOSE. Have you seen spirits?

SENOR ALLONES. Don't go insulting my intelligence. I am a communist.

DON JOSE. Still?

SENOR ALLONES. It's not that we weren't right, it's just that we didn't win.

DON JOSE. So what have you seen?

SENOR ALLONES. I have seen nothing that cannot be explained.

A pause. SENOR ALLONES considers his options. Finally, he decides to confess.

When I was rolling I felt someone standing at my shoulder. It made me slip the roll.

DON JOSE. A presence . . .

SENOR ALLONES. When I looked, there was no one there.

DON JOSE. Eyes staring at you.

SENOR ALLONES. Yes! Don Jose promise you will never reveal any of this to anyone. But I swear I heard . . .

DON JOSE. What did you hear?

SENOR ALLONES. A voice.

DON JOSE. An African woman.

SENOR ALLONES. Yes! And she told me . . .

DON JOSE. That you must tell me the truth.

SENOR ALLONES. That I must tell you a secret.

DON JOSE. What secret?

A long pause. SENOR ALLONES *seems reluctant to go on.*

Senor Allones, giving people unwelcome news has been one
of your favourite pastimes for thirty years. What's different
today?

Finally . . .

SENOR ALLONES. You will recall that on the rainy night when
Alexandra was born, my wife helped with the delivery.

DON JOSE. I understand she was extremely helpful. She
mixed rum with rainwater and eventually fainted.

SENOR ALLONES. Even so . . . she told me that when your
wife was in great pain she began to say things . . . about
Alexandra's father.

DON JOSE. Ah. Now I see.

SENOR ALLONES. Don Jose, did you ever try to work
backwards from the birth and calculate where you were on
the night of conception.

DON JOSE. I have refrained from mathematics.

SENOR ALLONES. This is biology.

DON JOSE. It is history.

SENOR ALLONES. So you lie to yourself.

DON JOSE. That is a feat I have never managed.

SENOR ALLONES. What I am saying is that in her moment of
pain, your wife suggested that Alexandra wasn't your child.

A pause.

DON JOSE. Would you like to smoke a cigar?

SENOR ALLONES. I am not allowed. My doctor is a woman.

DON JOSE. But she isn't here.

DON JOSE *takes out a cigar box and offers it to* SENOR ALLONES. *He hesitates before taking it.*

SENOR ALLONES. I am only raising this topic with you now, Don Jose, because . . .

DON JOSE. Because you are afraid of spirits.

DON JOSE *gets up to fetch matches.* SENOR ALLONES *talks to his back.*

SENOR ALLONES. You are an atheist, Don Jose?

As DON JOSE *returns he is deep in thought.*

DON JOSE. Decreasingly.

SENOR ALLONES. But the real secret, Don Jose, is this. I know who Alexandra's real father is.

DON JOSE *holds out his lit match. It burns down to his fingers while* SENOR ALLONES *waits for a response. A pause.* DON JOSE *blows out the match.*

DON JOSE (*softly*). So do I.

A pause. SENOR ALLONES *is about to speak but* DON JOSE *silences him with a single shake of the head.*

Let us return to silence.

SENOR ALLONES. Are you not even curious to speak to him about it?

DON JOSE. We speak to each other about it with our eyes only. Every day for twenty-one years.

A pause. SENOR ALLONES *shrugs and gets to his feet.*

SENOR ALLONES. So you are no better than the rest of us.

DON JOSE. And no worse.

SENOR ALLONES. If you don't mind, I will smoke this cigar later.

DON JOSE. I do mind. That cigar was meant for that moment.

SENOR ALLONES *stops and hands the cigar back to* DON JOSE.

SENOR ALLONES. So . . . we will return to not speaking to each other.

DON JOSE *raises his bottle of tequila in a toast.*

DON JOSE. To silence in the gulf between old enemies.

SENOR ALLONES *sets off to leave . . .*

Before we embark on another eight years, Senor Allones . . . purely in terms of tobacco. What do you think of Miguel Fernando?

SENOR ALLONES *shrugs.*

SENOR ALLONES. He is the best I've ever seen.

DON JOSE *nods.*

DON JOSE. We should try to save him.

SENOR ALLONES. Maybe.

SENOR ALLONES *leaves. He walks through the adjoining door into . . .*

The rolling room.

The rolling room is deserted and we can hear the noise of music coming from the courtyard. SENOR ALLONES *makes his way to* ALEXANDRA*'s bench and studies it. He then slowly bends down and picks up* ALEXANDRA*'s sandals. He pushes his fingers into the toe of one of the sandals. He looks around then puts the sandals back. He then hurriedly heads for the stairs which lead up to the attic room above, which is in darkness.*

After a few moments, SANCHO *enters from outside, bursting through the doors in his wheelchair. He wheels himself to the front of stage and parks beside* ALEXANDRA's *desk. He checks his watch and after a few moments,* DONA ALBINA *enters, hurrying.*

DONA ALBINA. I'm sorry I'm late. I now use the American method of brushing my teeth and it takes a long time. Is it all clear?

SANCHO. They are all dancing.

DONA ALBINA. Good. Shall we do it here?

SANCHO. Yes. Right here.

SANCHO *unbuttons his fly and* DONA ALBINA *kneels down beside him. She then leans over* SANCHO's *lap and although we cannot see the details, we infer that she is giving him a blow job.*

She pumps away for a few moments then stops and peers at SANCHO.

DONA ALBINA. What's wrong?

SANCHO *looks bashful.*

SANCHO. I think today . . . I am not in the mood.

DONA ALBINA *sits back on her haunches.*

DONA ALBINA. You're always in the mood. My God . . . what 'mood'?

SANCHO. Today I'm not in it.

DONA ALBINA. Well, I have to say . . . I think you are being pretty ungrateful.

SANCHO. I am not a beggar.

A pause.

DONA ALBINA. Sancho, can I remind you that our Wednesday sessions are the only truly charitable work I do all week? Without them I am an unremitting sinner and therefore doomed to perdition.

SANCHO. Dona Albina, I would do anything to help smuggle you into heaven but things like this are beyond a man's control.

A pause. DONA ALBINA *begins to pace around him.*

DONA ALBINA. Are you sick?

SANCHO. No.

DONA ALBINA. What then?

A pause.

SANCHO. Normally, Dona Albina . . . when you are . . . helping me . . . I think about Alexandra.

DONA ALBINA. Why, thank you.

SANCHO. But today when I think of her, I think of the fact that she has gone and that makes me think about the vacancy and that makes me think about my ambition to further my career.

DONA ALBINA. I think I know what is coming next.

A pause.

SANCHO. Dona Albina . . .

DONA ALBINA. Please don't.

SANCHO. I am simply asking that you speak to Don Silver . . .

DONA ALBINA. Do you think Don Silver listens to me? Do you think he cares about this place any more?

SANCHO. Then I will speak to Don Silver myself.

DONA ALBINA. Senor Silver is away on business.

SANCHO. I know. But soon he will return.

A pause. DONA ALBINA *hides her face from* SANCHO. *She has something to hide and changes the subject.*

DONA ALBINA. Am I old? Yes or no?

SANCHO. Where did he go on business?

DONA ALBINA. Mexico. Yucatan. Maybe that's why your cock won't work. Because I'm old. I have lost control.

A pause. SANCHO *seems to be deep in thought.*

SANCHO. When will he return?

DONA ALBINA. Who?

SANCHO. Don Silver!

   DONA ALBINA *still hides her face.*

DONA ALBINA. Why do you care?

SANCHO. Because I'm ambitious.

   A pause. DONA ALBINA *kneels down beside* SANCHO
   and addresses his penis directly.

DONA ALBINA. Well, Mr Cockerel? Yes or no?

SANCHO. Just tell me . . . right now, this second, when is Don
   Silver coming back to Cuba?

DONA ALBINA. Who knows? Anything can happen. Storms,
   terrorism, earthquakes. Who am I, God?

SANCHO. If God is busy elsewhere . . . then yes, you are.

DONA ALBINA. Just concentrate on my charity.

   DONA ALBINA *resumes her attempts at a blow job.*
   SANCHO *looks up at the ceiling.*

SANCHO. Lord, what is so wrong with a little bit of ambition?

   Suddenly ELENA *and* MARIA *burst into the rolling room
   from the courtyard, followed by the rest of the* WORKERS,
   all in uproar. DONA ALBINA *leaps to her feet and*
   SANCHO *hastily buttons his fly. Behind* ELENA *and*
   MARIA, *two other* WOMEN WORKERS *are carrying a
   very old black* WOMAN *into the rolling room. The*
   WOMAN *is wearing long flowing robes and a calico
   turban. She appears to be unconscious.*

DONA ALBINA (*wiping her mouth*). What the hell is going
   on?

MARIA. She fainted.

ELENA. I think she's dying . . .

CRISTINA *enjoys the melodrama.*

CRISTINA. She looks exactly how my grandmother looked when she died. First they go grey then white then that greeny colour they have on the Mexican flag.

SANCHO. Who is she?

ELENA. We don't know.

They sit the OLD WOMAN down and begin to fan her face. DONA ALBINA looks down at the WOMAN and gasps in shock. She puts her hand to her mouth then tries to hide her recognition. SENOR ALLONES has appeared from the attic room and is joining the throng. DON JOSE has wandered in from the maturing room to see what the noise is about. Also MIGUEL and SIMON are strolling to front of stage, amused and dubious.

MARIA. So what do we do? Is she dead?

DONA ALBINA (*softly*). No, she's not dead.

MARIA. She's breathing. Give her some air.

TIMPO. We should call a doctor.

DONA ALBINA. No, no it's OK. We can deal with it.

DON JOSE. What happened to her?

MARIA. We didn't see.

ELENA. We were all dancing. Then there was a bird . . .

MARIA. It was calling out . . .

ELENA. Then when the violinist stopped playing there was this old woman lying on the ground.

MARIA. I swear she dropped out of the sky.

DON JOSE (*suspicious*). What kind of bird was it?

MARIA. An owl.

ELENA. A crow.

MARIA. We all saw something different.

DON JOSE peers at DONA ALBINA. DONA ALBINA *lowers her head.* MIGUEL *is lighting a cigarette and stops as he notices the looks between them.*

MIGUEL. Dona Albina? Who is this woman?

A pause.

It's OK, Dona Albina, I'm not expecting a logical reply.

DON JOSE. Miguel Fernando! This is not the place to discuss this.

A pause. Everyone senses from DON JOSE*'s voice that all is not as it seems.* MIGUEL *smokes and persists . . .*

MIGUEL. Dona Albina, I am the President. Who is this woman?

A pause. DONA ALBINA *puts a handkerchief to her face, filled with trepidation.*

DONA ALBINA. She looks so exhausted.

She looks anxiously to DON JOSE.

Perhaps there was a storm.

SIMON. She's just a drunk, for Christ's sake.

DONA ALBINA. Shhhh.

DON JOSE. Gently, gently . . .

SIMON. Miguel?

DON JOSE. Let us take her to the tobacco room. It is cooler there. Miguel Fernando . . . help us.

SIMON *comes to* MIGUEL*'s shoulder. In the background* MARIA *and* ELENA *are also gathering courage to approach.*

SIMON. Miguel, what's the matter with you? Throw her out into the street.

MIGUEL. Who am I to throw anyone in the street?

SIMON. You are the boss.

MIGUEL. A compassionate one.

MARIA *and* ELENA *have arrived at* MIGUEL's *other shoulder.* MARIA *tugs his sleeve.*

MARIA. Miguel.

MARIA *gestures at the unconscious* WOMAN.

That woman is a spirit.

ELENA. You should get her out of here, boss.

SIMON. Miguel, it's fifteen minutes past. We should be working. We are all losing money.

SENOR ALLONES *checks his watch and calls out.*

SANCHO. Miguel has been in charge for half a day and already I have lost two hours' pay.

DON JOSE *and* MIGUEL *peer at each other.* DON JOSE *gestures at* MIGUEL *to speak up. Finally . . .*

MIGUEL. OK, all of you, get back to work. Simon, you finish the Lusitanias. Sancho . . . you can take the place of Alexandra.

SANCHO. For good?

MIGUEL. For now.

MARIA. What do we listen to?

MIGUEL. The beating of your own hearts.

DONA ALBINA, DON JOSE, MIGUEL *and the* OLD WOMAN *pass through the door into . . .*

The maturing room.

The lights fade up as DON JOSE *and* MIGUEL *help the* OLD WOMAN *towards the bales of tobacco. As they walk,* DONA ALBINA *sobs a little.*

DONA ALBINA. What time did Alexandra's boat leave last night?

DON JOSE *and* DONA ALBINA *look to* MIGUEL.

MIGUEL (*guilty*). I don't remember.

DONA ALBINA. Didn't you even say goodbye?

MIGUEL. I tried to make her stay.

DON JOSE. And you failed. The boat will have left at high tide. Midnight.

DONA ALBINA. Then it's possible that the storm that spoiled the tobacco caught up with her boat.

They settle the OLD WOMAN *down, using bales of tobacco as a couch.*

DON JOSE. We won't know until she wakes.

DONA ALBINA *kneels beside the* OLD WOMAN *and uses a damp cloth to wipe her face.* DON JOSE *kneels on the other side of her. The scene is lit by a shaft of light and looks like something from the Old Testament.* MIGUEL *folds his arms and peers at them.*

MIGUEL. Very pretty. I should take a photograph.

DONA ALBINA. She wouldn't be visible on any photograph. She would just be a . . .

MIGUEL. Miasma?

DONA ALBINA. Yes. (*A pause.*) What's a miasma?

MIGUEL *shakes his head in disbelief.*

MIGUEL. If you want to wake her up, why don't you wave a fifty-dollar note under her nose?

DONA ALBINA (*to* DON JOSE). My guess is that she has flown here from the Gulf.

MIGUEL. My guess is that she can hear every word we are saying.

DON JOSE. Miguel, if you are going to hide from what you already know to be true, you should leave now. You will only cause us harm.

MIGUEL *chuckles to himself, holds his eyes closed with his fingertips. The* OLD WOMAN *stirs a little then settles back to sleep.* MIGUEL *hoots with laughter.*

DONA ALBINA. She is fighting against something very powerful.

MIGUEL. The desire to laugh out loud.

DON JOSE (*softly*). We should burn tobacco.

DONA ALBINA. Yes! An offering.

DON JOSE *hurries to a small humidor and begins to sort through particular cigar boxes.* MIGUEL *watches him with disgust.*

MIGUEL. This morning, Don Jose, I thought you were as good a rational atheist as I have ever known.

DON JOSE. That was before my daughter put herself at the mercy of the four winds.

MIGUEL. So check the weather reports on the radio.

DON JOSE *turns.*

DON JOSE. Do we still roll Especiales here, Miguel?

MIGUEL. What has that got to do with it?

DON JOSE. Yes or no?

MIGUEL. We stopped.

DON JOSE. Why?

MIGUEL. Because Don Pedro died.

DON JOSE. They were the best cigars you made.

MIGUEL *is a little thrown.*

You stopped making Especiales because you thought Don Pedro's spirit would not approve. Do you have any in the humidor?

A pause.

MIGUEL. I burnt them all.

DON JOSE. So . . .

MIGUEL. What do you mean, 'so'?

DON JOSE. You are as much of a rationalist as I am.

MIGUEL *lets out a yelp of laughter.*

MIGUEL. That is not the same as letting some peasant midwife with a bone in her nose fleece you for half your savings in return for some fumbling performance of African superstitions.

DON JOSE. Who are you trying to convince, Miguel?

DONA ALBINA *can hardly hear* MIGUEL *and looks to* DON JOSE.

DONA ALBINA. We have to pray that she is stronger than the storm . . .

MIGUEL. Dona Albina, are you taking medication?

DONA ALBINA. A little, for my nerves.

MIGUEL. Then may I suggest you increase the dose. And Don Jose, perhaps you need to renew your acquaintanceship with cause and effect.

DON JOSE. Miguel, why don't you go and find enough opium to shut your fucking mouth.

MIGUEL *reacts and at that moment* SIMON *enters, carrying a large cigar. He reacts to the sight of the sleeping* WOMAN *and hesitates.*

MIGUEL (*sharply*). What do you want?

SIMON *glances at* DON JOSE *and then holds out the cigar to* MIGUEL.

SIMON. My first Lusitania. Is it OK?

DON JOSE *stares at* MIGUEL *as he takes the cigar and examines it for a few moments. He then drops it on the floor and grinds it with his foot before setting off for . . .*

The rolling room.

The WORKERS *are all hard at work as* MIGUEL *enters.*
SANCHO *wheels himself closer to* ALEXANDRA*'s bench to
secure his position.*

SIMON *follows on* MIGUEL*'s heels.*

SIMON. Miguel!

MIGUEL. The Lusitania is for Kings and Presidents.

SIMON (*angry*). You're freezing up, Miguel. In July.

   MIGUEL *turns sharply and addresses the factory.*

MIGUEL. For entertainment this afternoon we are going to
   listen to the radio.

SENOR ALLONES. We don't want any more music!

SIMON. I thought you wanted silence!

   MIGUEL *goes to the radio cassette player and begins to
   tune it on radio frequencies.*

MIGUEL. There will be no more silence!

   We hear loud white-noise and static as MIGUEL *feverishly
   searches the frequencies. We hear American stations of all
   types – Rock and Roll, Country, Religious – all sampled in
   one-second bursts between waves of static.*

SENOR ALLONES. You have lost your mind, Miguel.

MARIA. Turn it off!

SIMON. What are you looking for?

MIGUEL. An American weather report.

SANCHO. He has lost his mind.

   *The sudden bursts of American stations become more
   frantic.*

MARIA. Turn it off, Miguel!

   We hear the word 'news' amidst the hiss.

MIGUEL. News from America . . . there. Soon they'll tell us the weather.

We hear the briefest snippet of a news bulletin which is soon swallowed in static. MIGUEL curses and begins to re-tune the radio. The static howls. Finally, SENOR ALLONES, who is the only one still rolling, looks up.

SENOR ALLONES (*calmly*). If you turn that thing off, I will give you the weather report.

TIMPO enters, his bright mood clashing with the tension in the room.

TIMPO. Weather report? It's summer, there is no weather. Just heat and dust and rats.

TIMPO sees MIGUEL and SENOR ALLONES' look of seriousness and stops. MIGUEL turns the radio off.

MIGUEL (*to SENOR ALLONES*). What do you mean?

SENOR ALLONES. I know the way the weather works. My father was a fisherman.

A pause. Everyone waits and SENOR ALLONES relishes the moment. He pronounces with great professionalism . . .

Last night there was a storm in Havana.

SANCHO. That is amazing.

SIMON. The man is a fucking genius.

SENOR ALLONES. Storms head north and west.

SANCHO. How does he know this shit?

SENOR ALLONES. I told you, my father was a fisherman.

TIMPO. You knew your father?

SIMON. Our theories were wrong.

MIGUEL. Fucking shut up! All of you! (*A pause.*) Let him speak.

MARIA. Oh yes, Sir boss.

A pause.

SENOR ALLONES. Storms head north and west from Cuba.

MIGUEL. How fast?

SENOR ALLONES. Faster than a boat.

MIGUEL. If a boat left at midnight last night.

SENOR ALLONES. What time did the storm hit Havana?

SANCHO. You didn't hear it?

SENOR ALLONES. I'm deaf.

SIMON. Two a.m. It woke my father's chickens.

MIGUEL. So if the boat was heading towards Key West when would the storm catch them?

SENOR ALLONES *looks at his watch.*

SENOR ALLONES. An hour ago.

A pause. MIGUEL stares at SENOR ALLONES and knows that he is speaking the truth. The silent tension is broken by a giggle and a whisper . . .

MARIA (*softly*). We're talking about Alexandra's boat, right?

CRISTINA. Of course!

ELENA. Shhhhh.

MARIA crosses herself. A pause.

SENOR ALLONES. But you shouldn't worry about her, Miguel. It's going to be OK.

SANCHO (*incredulous*). What did he say?

SENOR ALLONES. Alexandra is on board a good boat. The boat will survive the storm.

SANCHO. I don't believe it! After ten years the old bastard has said something optimistic.

SIMON. How do you know it's a good boat?

SANCHO. Because his father was a fisherman.

SIMON. He didn't even see the fucking boat.

SENOR ALLONES. I didn't have to. I knew already.

A pause. All eyes are on SENOR ALLONES *and he's even happier than before. He begins to roll a cigar. Finally, he speaks, matter-of-factly . . .*

If it was just some smuggler's junk, it would sink. But it's an expensive boat. When Don Silver buys a boat he makes sure it is a good one.

A pause. It takes a while for this to resonate. MIGUEL *turns.*

MIGUEL. What do you mean, 'When Don Silver buys a boat'?

SENOR ALLONES *looks all around with mock surprise.*

SENOR ALLONES. You didn't know? None of you?

SIMON. Know what?

SENOR ALLONES. Alexandra sailed to America on board Don Silver's boat.

SIMON. He is drunk.

SANCHO. He always says whatever he thinks will hurt the most.

SENOR ALLONES (*shrugging*). How can that hurt anyone? I am saying that it is a good boat. I am saying that Alexandra will survive.

SIMON. Why would Don Silver give Alexandra a boat?

The old man pauses then looks around at them all again and begins to chuckle to himself.

SENOR ALLONES. You all talk as if you are so clever but you are all so stupid.

SIMON. Miguel, it's OK. Stay calm.

SENOR ALLONES. I am officially deaf, so I hear more than the rest of you. Things I am not supposed to hear. In storerooms, barns, offices. And besides, I see things you don't see. Tiny gestures. The way two people look into each other's eyes.

SANCHO. He's lying.

SENOR ALLONES. Alexandra and Don Silver are both on board that boat. They are going to America to live together.

A pause.

MARIA. Mother of God.

ELENA. That's disgusting!

SENOR ALLONES. What is disgusting is that the owner of this factory is never coming back. So Miguel really is the President and this place will go to hell.

There is silence. Dumb shock. MIGUEL *gets to his feet.*

MIGUEL. You're a fucking liar!

SENOR ALLONES. Ask Dona Albina. Ask her when Don Silver is coming back.

MARIA *and* ELENA *are on their feet.*

MARIA. But he's so old.

SENOR ALLONES. And so rich.

MARIA *(firmly)*. No one is rich and no one is poor.

SENOR ALLONES. Oh my sweet innocent virgin.

SANCHO *looks all around.*

SANCHO. That's insane. He would never leave all this behind!

SENOR ALLONES *laughs and gets to his feet. He opens his arms to encompass the whole factory.*

SENOR ALLONES. All what!? In five years' time we will be sitting at these benches putting batteries into toy plastic monkeys for two Yankee dollars a day.

MIGUEL *grabs his chaveta and suddenly leaps towards* SENOR ALLONES *but is restrained by* SIMON. SENOR ALLONES *brandishes his chaveta too.*

I would have told you sooner but it made me laugh to see you dragging your heart all over the factory.

MIGUEL *tries once again to get at* SENOR ALLONES *but* SIMON *and* TIMPO *combine to pull him back.* SIMON *peels his fingers from the chaveta. There is silence. Finally,* SENOR ALLONES *shrugs.*

What do you expect, Miguel? What do you have?

A pause. MARIA *raises her hand.*

MARIA. Love, Miguel. Tell him love.

SENOR ALLONES. Twenty years ago at midnight, my wife got on board a boat to Key West. She left me here with three children. All night long I prayed her boat would sink. That is love. How does it feel, Miguel Fernando?

A pause. The lights fade in the rolling room as the lights fade up in . . .

The maturing room.

DON JOSE *and* DONA ALBINA *are playing chess beside the sleeping body of the* VOODOO DOCTOR, *killing time. Candles flicker all around.* DON JOSE *makes a move.*

DON JOSE. You should have told me sooner.

DONA ALBINA. Told you what?

DON JOSE. That you were carrying my child.

DONA ALBINA. What would you have done if I'd told you?

DON JOSE. What any decent Cuban man would do. Build a raft and head for Miami.

DONA ALBINA *smiles. A pause.* DON JOSE *makes a move on the chess board.*

And yet . . . I would have liked to have had a child of my own. A child that really was mine.

DONA ALBINA *looks up at him. A long pause.*

Please don't pretend you don't know, Dona Albina. We are in the presence of the voodoo. We must speak the truth.

DONA ALBINA. The voodoo is asleep. We can make do with half the truth.

A pause. DONA ALBINA *puts her handkerchief to her eyes.*

Let the voodoo sleep a little longer.

Suddenly the door flies open from the rolling room and MIGUEL *enters in a rage. He yells.*

MIGUEL. Dona Albina! Tell me when Don Silver is coming back!

DON JOSE. Miguel, be quiet, she is sleeping.

MIGUEL. Tell me!

DONA ALBINA *glances back at the sleeping* WOMAN.

DONA ALBINA. You must be careful with these people, Miguel, they have been here since before Columbus.

MIGUEL *sweeps some candles from a bale of tobacco.*

MIGUEL. I don't care about this voodoo shit! Tell me where he is!

A pause. MIGUEL *is panting hard.* DONA ALBINA *glances at the* VOODOO WOMAN *who stirs a little.* DON JOSE *takes her hand.*

DON JOSE. It's not your fault if the truth causes unhappiness.

DONA ALBINA. Don Silver is on the boat with Alexandra.

MIGUEL *glares at them both, murder in his eyes.*

MIGUEL. When that old bitch wakes, tell her I will pay her double if she can make the boat sink.

MIGUEL *storms back towards the rolling room.* DONA ALBINA *goes to follow him but* DON JOSE *stops her. Lights fade.*

The rolling room.

Lights fade up as MIGUEL *enters. Everyone is hard at work but they stop as he storms into the room.*

MIGUEL. Old man! Remind me who is in charge here today.

SENOR ALLONES *stands and bows with mock reverence.*

SENOR ALLONES. You are, oh Presidente.

MIGUEL. Then I order you all to go home!

SIMON. Miguel, please . . .

MIGUEL. Go home! Right now.

SENOR ALLONES. We don't obey insane orders.

MIGUEL. Today is President's Day. It's my birthday. It's the anniversary of the revolution. Now fuck off.

SANCHO. Miguel, there are directors. When the news gets out about Don Silver, there will be a directors' meeting.

MIGUEL *leaps up on his desk and yells.*

MIGUEL. Today this factory belongs to me! And I order you all to go home! This day is over!

MARIA *and* ELENA *swap looks, shrug and get to their feet. Other* WORKERS *follow suit and begin to grab their belongings.* SENOR ALLONES *smiles as he gets to his feet.*

SENOR ALLONES. It is as I predicted.

SIMON. Shut your mouth!

They watch SENOR ALLONES *put on his straw hat and blazer.*

SENOR ALLONES. You can't blame me for any of this. I only shed light. In Cuba, with light comes heat.

He leaves. SANCHO *laughs nervously . . .*

SANCHO. Miguel Fernando, I thought this was a democracy. Don't we even get to vote?

MIGUEL *gestures at the* WORKERS, *who are now hurriedly departing.*

MIGUEL. They are voting.

A pause. Now only SANCHO *and* SIMON *are staying put as everyone else packs up to go. Finally,* SANCHO *prepares to leave.*

SANCHO. So Miguel, are you going to recommend that I take Alexandra's place?

MIGUEL *looks at* SANCHO *and after a few moments begins to laugh.*

MIGUEL. Now that is good. That is an appropriate exchange. Don't you think, Simon?! We replace Don Quixote with Sancho Panza. In place of my love, we now have a crippled veteran of a pointless war.

SIMON. Miguel!

*SANCHO *glares and then makes a decision. He begins to turn to wheel himself towards the exit.*

Sancho, wait . . .

SANCHO. It's OK, Simon. I don't hear him. He's just a little kid. And Miguel . . . if anybody around here is a cripple . . . it's you.

Now it's just MIGUEL *and* SIMON. SIMON *steps a little closer. He laughs, bewildered . . . desperate to defuse the situation. A long pause. Finally . . .*

SIMON. You want some coffee?

SIMON *goes to the percolator and pours two cups as* MIGUEL *sits down at his desk.* SIMON *puts the cup in front of him.*

So how did I do? Helping you through the day. Out of ten? Zero?

MIGUEL *doesn't answer.*

Hey . . . we can still go out tonight. We said we'd go out tonight, remember?

MIGUEL *turns to* SIMON *and studies him.*

MIGUEL. Ah yes. We were going to go hunting. For what, Simon? You didn't say.

SIMON *shrugs, embarrassed.*

SIMON. What do you think?

MIGUEL. Tell me.

SIMON *hesitates, grins . . .*

SIMON. Girls.

MIGUEL. Girls? You want to go hunting for girls?

MIGUEL *shakes his head with weary disgust.*

Today you should tell the truth.

SIMON *burns with embarrassment.*

SIMON. About what, Miguel?

MIGUEL. Ah to hell with it.

SIMON. To hell with what?

MIGUEL. It doesn't matter, my friend.

A pause. SIMON *grins . . .*

SIMON. What did you mean? Jesus Christ!

MIGUEL. That's three. I counted. Your tongue is tin.

SIMON. Come on, Miguel.

MIGUEL. Let's go to Rikki's bar and split a bottle of rum.

SIMON. I want to know what truth you are talking about.

A pause. MIGUEL *chuckles.*

MIGUEL. Simon, it's been a hard day. Let's preserve some secrets.

SIMON. You think you know something.

MIGUEL. Silence. I choose silence.

SIMON. I choose relief from suspense.

MIGUEL. Simon, you don't like to fuck girls. It's OK.

A pause. SIMON *turns his back on* MIGUEL.

Simon, who cares.

SIMON. Is that a question?

MIGUEL. How long have we been friends?

SIMON *turns.*

SIMON. You know, Miguel, today . . .

MIGUEL. Today what?

SIMON. Today you failed.

MIGUEL. Failed what?

SIMON. You had power and you threw it away.

MIGUEL. Power? What the fuck do I want with power?

SIMON. In one day you hurt everyone.

MIGUEL. Simon, look, I'm sorry . . .

SIMON. Alexandra left because she knew if she stayed around you, she would become a junkie too.

MIGUEL (*sudden anger*). OK, Simon, the truth. It's me you want to fuck. Yes or no?

A long pause. SIMON*'s eyes fill with tears. Then he finds some resolve. Finally . . .*

SIMON. Not any more, Miguel.

SIMON *grabs his coat, turns and heads for the exit. On the way out he bows to the portrait of Castro.* MIGUEL *is left alone.*

He begins to wander through the empty benches. He peers up at Castro and at Partagas. He then makes a decision. He goes to some bales of tobacco and shoves them out of the way. He reaches into a recess and produces a small cellophane bag of white powder. He brings it quickly to his desk. MIGUEL *lights a match and begins to cook the heroin on a twist of silver foil buried in the powder. He spits on the foil and then waits a few moments. Soon a thick white smoke begins to rise from the cooked heroin and* MIGUEL *breathes it in deeply. He takes three or four huge breaths and then sits back a little.*

MIGUEL. Snow. She wanted snow, I've got snow. Beautiful, beautiful white snow.

He picks up her sandals from beneath her desk and addresses them.

Alexandra, do you want to play in it? You want me to bury you in it? Up to your neck? Higher? Over your beautiful head. Drown in it. All they find is your sandals. Washed up on the beach. Let the Americans have your body. Do what they want with it.

MIGUEL *gets to his feet and yells.*

Hey Alexandra! You can do Cuba's latest dance. The Guantanamo Bay Tango.

MIGUEL *begins to shuffle along as if his hands and ankles were bound by chains.*

You like that dance, Alexandra? Why the fuck did you go to America when America has already come to us?!

A pause. After a few moments the door to the factory opens and in a shaft of light the VIOLINIST *appears. He walks into the factory and stands facing* MIGUEL. MIGUEL *straightens up and laughs.*

What? We forgot to pay you?

MIGUEL *reaches into his pockets and begins to search for change. He giggles to himself.*

It would have been more profitable, my friend, if you had stuck to playing in the street for the tourists. The ones who say to us 'well done' for being so poor and so brave.

He counts out some coins.

You think they're putting their hands on their hearts when they swear they support our struggle. What they're really doing is putting their hands on their wallets to make sure we don't steal them.

MIGUEL *produces some coins and takes them over to the*
VIOLINIST. *He puts them in the* VIOLINIST'*s hand but
after a moment, the* VIOLINIST *lets the coins drop to the
ground.*

What's the matter? Are you drunk? Maybe you'd like
something stronger.

MIGUEL *holds up the bag of heroin and shakes it. The*
VIOLINIST *puts his violin to his shoulder and begins to
play a mournful Cuban ballad.*

No, no, I don't want you to play.

The VIOLINIST *plays on.*

There is no one here to listen to you.

The music continues.

I want silence! Didn't you hear? I am the President!

The music plays faster.

I gave you an order! There will be no music in this factory
any more . . .

He yells.

. . . because we . . . voted for . . . silence!!!

The VIOLINIST *stops playing. As he does,* DON JOSE
enters from the maturing room. DON JOSE *walks by the*
VIOLINIST *and dismisses him with a nod of the head.
The* VIOLINIST *bows and then heads for the door. As he
leaves . . .*

DON JOSE. It's OK, Miguel. He isn't real.

MIGUEL *watches the* VIOLINIST *leave, then gestures at
the maturing room.*

MIGUEL. Has she woken yet?

DON JOSE *doesn't answer. Instead he examines the silver
foil on* MIGUEL'*s desk.* MIGUEL *is angered by his look of
contempt.*

Please don't look at me like that. You knew about Alexandra
and Don Silver, right?

DON JOSE *doesn't answer.*

But you let the boss have her because you didn't want to
lose your fucking job.

DON JOSE *is now analysing* MIGUEL*'s bag of white
powder, sniffing it with disgust.*

Didn't it bother you to think of a man older than you
fucking her. She's bent over . . . waiting . . . waiting . . .
'Come on, old man, get the fucking thing hard.' Wondering
what she has to do. Does she have to suck the shrivelled-up
ghost of a cock to get it to operate?

DON JOSE. Are you really so angry you want the boat to
sink?

MIGUEL. Sink down to hell!

DON JOSE. If I told you Don Silver isn't Alexandra's lover . . .
that he is her father.

A pause. MIGUEL *stares at* DON JOSE *in disbelief.* DON
JOSE *smiles.*

True. Voodoo.

MIGUEL *hesitates then laughs it off.*

MIGUEL. You are Alexandra's father.

DON JOSE *shakes his head.*

DON JOSE. I only raised her. With love. Like a field of
tobacco. But I always knew the truth. My wife had her
affairs and I had mine. She said it was like eating oranges
with someone.

DON JOSE *is filled with bitter regret.*

I told Alexandra the truth two months ago on her twenty-
first birthday. Someone should have warned me. Some
voice. Don't play with that. Don't play with 'true' and 'not
true'. You think love can compete with biology? You think
it's even a contest?

A pause.

So you see, Miguel, Alexandra wasn't leaving you. She was leaving me. But even so . . . I never wanted that damned boat to sink.

A pause. DON JOSE*'s eyes fill with tears . . .*

I really didn't want it to happen. I even prayed to a God who I don't believe in. I offered tobacco . . .

A pause.

But still . . . the boat did sink. (*A pause.*) The boat did sink.

MIGUEL *reacts.*

MIGUEL. What are you talking about?

DON JOSE *gestures through to the maturing room.*

DON JOSE. She woke up and told us that the boat was lost.

A pause.

MIGUEL. And you believe her?

DON JOSE *sits down at* ALEXANDRA's *desk and begins to sob.*

Don Jose! Have you lost your mind? You are taking the word of a voodoo doctor?

MIGUEL *laughs.*

Don Jose, she will be ashore by now. She will be in a pink hotel . . . she will be drinking a cocktail called . . . 'Moonlight on the Water'.

DON JOSE *slams his fist on the desk.*

DON JOSE. I will not tolerate false hope.

MIGUEL. Logic, Don Jose! Reason! Why are you crying when there is no reason to cry?!

The door to the maturing room opens and DONA ALBINA *appears, holding a handkerchief to her face.* MIGUEL *heads for the door.*

I want to speak to that old bitch!

DONA ALBINA *stands in* MIGUEL's *way.*

DONA ALBINA. She's gone.

MIGUEL. Gone where?

DON JOSE. Back into the tobacco.

DONA ALBINA *takes* DON JOSE *by the arm and helps him to his feet.* MIGUEL *steps back towards his desk. He glances at the burnt remains of the heroin on the desk.*

MIGUEL. This is all smoke.

MIGUEL *shakes his bag of white powder at them.*

You are both snow.

DONA ALBINA. Then you must listen to us before we melt.

MIGUEL. She is alive. Even if the boat was capsized she could swim the last few yards.

DONA ALBINA *and* DON JOSE *help each other towards the exit of the factory.* MIGUEL *half-follows them, yelling.*

She's in a hotel room. Sitting on the balcony. Looking south at the horizon and thinking of you, Don Jose. And you, Dona Albina.

DONA ALBINA. Tomorrow I will sing you a song, Miguel.

They continue to depart. MIGUEL *turns to his desk and babbles . . .*

MIGUEL. This is smoke. It's OK, it's OK. I'm asleep on my desk. This whole day has been smoke.

He turns back to them and yells . . .

I'm going to wait right here, OK? I will wait for her to call. Don Jose, you said she would call when she reached America. I will wait all night if I have to!

DON JOSE *and* DONA ALBINA *leave and close the door behind them. The factory is dark again.* MIGUEL FERNANDO *watches them go, then slumps down at his desk. He looks all around.*

At last. My ambition fulfilled. The President of an empty room.

After a moment, he gets to his feet. He looks down at the bag of white powder. He then grabs a leaf of tobacco, which he crushes and holds to his nose. He relishes the aroma of it and looks up at the portrait of Fidel Castro.

She is safe. She will call. I know she will call. Fidel . . . we have logic and we have reason on our side.

He bows then straightens. He sits back down at his desk and waits. He stares straight ahead for a long time. The door from the maturing room opens and the VOODOO DOCTOR *emerges. She walks slowly towards the exit of the factory, treading silently.* MIGUEL *doesn't hear her and doesn't turn. In a shaft of light, without turning, the* VOODOO DOCTOR *raises her hand with a grand gesture. As she does, a telephone begins to ring. As it rings,* MIGUEL *stares straight ahead, only his face betraying his emotion. The phone continues to ring as the curtain begins to fall.*

The End.